The Cross

Functional

Business:

Beyond Teams

Lisa Woods

INTRODUCTION

The Cross Functional Business is a book about building the mindset of an organization through constructive dialog that drives innovation, accountability and growth company-wide.

It's a teambuilding exercise, a communication exercise, a goal setting exercise, as well as a tool for career growth.

Best of all...it's simple to understand and easy to implement.

Whether you are a...

- **Business leader** interested in focusing your entire organization to work better as a team,
- **Departmental leader** looking to improve the level of service your group provides to the organization,
- **Or an individual** looking to understand how the overall business functions and how your own efforts can make a valuable impact.

...this book is a great tool for you.

CONTENTS

I
BENEFITS OF THE CROSS FUNCTIONAL BUSINESS

Cross Functional *Teams* have been around for a while. They're a popular way to engage individuals from various parts of the organization to collectively focus on a strategic initiative. Why do Cross Functional Teams exist? They exist to get people to work creatively, cooperatively and cohesively toward a common goal. They take people out of silos created by company structure and force them to work together as a team on important issues that need input from multiple functional business areas. These individuals don't give up their day jobs…instead, teamwork is in addition to their current responsibilities.

We know cross functional *thinking* breeds ideas and creativity- so why limit it to strategic projects? Pockets of collaboration aren't enough. *The Cross Functional Business* brings collaboration and accountability to the entire organization's daily life. Competitive, successful companies need to run this way all the time. So why isn't this way of working natural and commonplace? Let's take a look at *four common business structures* that get in our way.

1: Tightly Held Ownership Structure

Description: One business leader/owner directing all aspects of the organization typically in smaller privately held businesses.

Pros: Owner's passion and skill set, which initially grew the business, is maintained and continues to drive the business forward.

Cons: The business loses value if the owner steps away. The rest of the organization does not have the experience to function on its own.

2: Functional 'Silo' Structure

Description: One business leader with functional leaders reporting to him/her.

Pros: Direction and strategy are agreed to and pushed through each functional silo to implement. Skills and efficiency within each silo are the result of the functional leader's ability to develop and build their team.

Cons: Each functional silo feels ownership in what they control, but often separate their success from the other functions. This separation creates barriers that inhibit the success of a common business goal.

3: Divisional Structure

Description: Companies can create entire organizations (divisions) to focus activities on a specific geography, customer group or product line.

Pros: Each division can focus on meeting the needs of their market; differentiating themselves to be competitive and responsive.

Cons: There tends to be a lot of duplication of resources and costs doing business this way. Divisional leaders lose focus of other divisions and often the common collective goal.

4: Matrix Structure

Description: This is a 'shared resource' structure that is a hybrid between traditional *Divisional* and *Functional* structures.

Pros: Allows the business to maintain Divisional focus on a customer group or region while 'sharing' redundant resources across all parts of the overall company. The goal being to implement best practice of functional areas across the business while reducing costs.

Cons: Unlike traditional structures where direct line reporting accountability exists, Matrix organizations overlap leadership and accountability with two, sometimes three dotted line reports. This causes confusion, resource disputes and often power struggles.

No matter the business structure, the structure itself naturally dictates communication channels and the flow of information. These channels are limited by the 'Cons' represented above.

For example, in a Tightly Held Ownership Structure the owner controls the communication and is the focal point of all dialog. In a Functional Silo Structure communication flows through each silo based on the effectiveness of the silo itself and independent of how the other silos function. In Divisional Structures communication flows differently through each division and often differently through each functional silo within each division. And in Matrix Organizations communication can flow differently across shared resources on top of the flow of the Functional and Divisional communication channels that already exist.

It's exhausting just trying to explain it! No wonder it's often a major cause of employee dissatisfaction, turnover and inefficiencies within an organization. Let's be clear…Organization Structure is not to blame, however the flow of communication *as a direct result of organizational structure* does cause a negative impact on the entire business…employee engagement, innovation and profitability.

Cross functional teams were created to bridge the communication gap between functional business areas in an effort to achieve a common objective. Objectives typically defined as a project or initiative important to the company. However these teams are a microcosm of the business and do NOT hold the overall business accountable for anything. Conversely, The Cross Functional Business does just that. It brings clarity and accountability across the ENTIRE business, building a more agile organization that engages employees at all levels, fosters innovation, improves efficiencies and increases profits.

The Cross Functional Business is defined by a clearly articulated and shared *mindset* for how business will be conducted within each area of the company (functional, divisional, matrix or otherwise). It establishes job expectations and communication standards not only that each individual and/or group *commit to*, but are also held *accountable for* by all others.

The Cross Functional Business breaks down communication barriers to allow for an agile organization that can…

- Respond to market needs

4

- Communicate ideas and ensure they come to fruition

- Provide cohesive 'intel' to make decisions quickly and with cross functional buy-in

- Maximize resources, professional and monetary, based on a collective strategic focus

- Energize a culture of ownership and pride throughout the workforce by being heard and respected for bringing value to the overall team

Really this stuff works...so why isn't it commonplace? Because great communication is difficult to replicate as information passes through an organization. The more people an organization has, the more structure it has...the more difficult it becomes.

Similar to the children's game of whispering something in the next person's ear, and so on down the line, the more people involved in the flow of the message, the more distorted the message becomes once it gets to the end of the line. Imagine an organization that figures out a way to keep that message in tact verses one that loses its meaning as information flows through the business. Which one do you think has a higher likelihood to succeed?

Clearly any skilled communicator has an advantage in their career, and any business that communicates skillfully throughout its workforce has the advantage in their marketplace. By establishing Cross Functional Business practices in your company, you are providing the tools to foster that skillful communication.

It can start with one individual that builds cross-functional connections. It can start with a functional group expanding its connections across silos, or it can start from the management team and filtered company wide. However you begin the process, it is sure to become infectious, as the obvious benefits are measured and shared.

II
HOW TO USE THIS BOOK

Step One: Read the book from start to finish.

Read all aspects of the book including functional areas that may not typically apply to you today. The Cross Functional Business begins with a Cross Functional *Mindset*. You'll be able to build this Mindset through understanding how each functional area *should* be interacting and communicating within, and outside, of structural company barriers. You will quickly begin to develop a new mindset for what your own Cross Functional Business should look like.

Step Two: Rate your organization's cross-functional activity as it stands today.

The survey at the end of the book takes everything you learn about The Cross Functional Business and allows you to rate your organization as doing something well, needing improvement or explain why that particular subject does not apply to your business at all.

It's important to define if an area does not apply so that you can think through it, and, if sharing your views with others, can discuss or debate the importance. As you make improvements in your organization, your perspective may evolve.

Step Three: Develop an action plan for 'needs improvement' areas of your business.

Some areas may be within your immediate control; others are great conversation starters with functional departments you work with. Use this tool to have that conversation and develop a better way of working, one that is defined for you to understand, adapt to, and share with others.

Step Four: Meet with your team and share the book.

As you share the book with your team, have them each conduct steps one-thee on their own. Next, regroup at a set time/date to discuss and collaborate on a collective *team* survey.

By having team members think through the process individually at first, each will be prepared to discuss issues and different perspectives during the team sit down. Make sure you have someone available to document the results and build an official report/plan that you can go back to over time and review continuous improvements.

This is a great team building exercise and offsite meeting discussion.

Step Five: Follow through on improvements.

Continue to share results and rate your progress as you follow through on areas needing improvement. Include results as part of your regular reports such as monthly or quarterly business reviews, or as part of your strategic planning process.

Step Six: Keep sharing, teaching and building the Cross Functional Mindset at all levels and areas of your organization.

This continuous improvement activity will set the tone for how your company does business. Document your company's Shared Mindset, Job Expectations and Communication Standards so they are accessible for the entire organization to read, understand, act upon and be held accountable for. Just as a standard operating procedure, The Cross Functional Business needs to be taught, referenced and measured. It is a living breathing system that should be documented & made real.

Step Seven: Customize the content based on your business structure.

Depending on how your business is set up, you may want to add R&D, Change Management, Legal Department or Distribution, for example, to your list of functional Job Expectation and Communication Standards. Remember, this is meant to improve communication flow and accountability based on your business structure, so don't leave anyone out!

Step Eight: Finally, don't give up.

Whether you influence change as an individual, functional manager or business leader, positive impact takes time and repetition. Your actions will improve the business on any scale…and your results will not go unnoticed!

III

3 KEY COMPONENTS: SHARED MINDSET, JOB EXPECTATIONS & COMMUNICATION STANDARDS

There are three key components to a successful Cross Functional Business.

1) Building a *Shared Mindset* for each functional area of the business:

- This is a general description of each function's realistic role in the overall business. Not only understood by the functional team, but by all other functional areas of the company.

2) Setting clear *Job Expectations* for individuals working in each functional area of the business:

- Job expectations are designed to guide people working within each functional area to do their jobs, as well as educate the rest of the business on what can be expected from the people working in each functional area.

3) Creating *Communication Standards* for each functional business area:

- Communication standards are ongoing dialog that should occur from, and with, each functional group. This can include communication reports designed to track useful information and progress throughout the organization. Communication is described within the Job Expectations section, not as a separate item. This is an important aspect of a successful Cross Functional Business. You cannot meet job expectations if you communicate poorly…the two go hand in hand.

Clarity Breeds Success

By documenting all three components you are essentially building a Standard Operating Procedure (S.O.P) for your Cross Functional Business. This S.O.P. serves as a tool your organization can use to:

- Train/retrain employees at all levels on how the business *should* work together.

- Educate employees and coworkers on the value each functional area brings to the *collective* team.

- Open the door to communication by lifting the veil off departmental silos, promoting discussion & access to information.

- Innovate throughout the organization by using a cross functional perspective to achieve not only project goals, but also day-to-day business improvements.

- Hold individuals, teams & managers accountable for working cross functionally.

- Grow your business with an innovative, accountable workforce that knows how to communicate and move together toward achieving a common goal.

Working together toward a common goal is the key to success in any business. Sure there are individuals, teams and often entire departments that function this way, but until the entire business is on track, roadblocks to innovation and growth are bound to exist. The Cross Functional Business bridges the communication gap allowing the ENTIRE business to work together.

IV
11 FUNCTIONAL AREAS THAT DRIVE INNOVATION, ACCOUNTABILITY & GROWTH ACROSS THE ENTIRE ORGANIZATION

Every business is different, however there are 11 Functional Areas common to most. These areas develop the core of The Cross Functional Business S.O.P.

Accounting; Customer Service; Finance; Human Resources; Information Technology; Marketing & Communications; Operations; Project Management; Purchasing & Supply Chain; Quality & Safety; Sales

As you read through each, ask yourself: Does this, or should this, apply to my organization?

ACCOUNTING

Shared Mindset

The Accounting Profession is an organization of checks and balances, but that is not all. Accounting also provides services to the sales organization, operations, purchasing team and all levels of management. The accounting organization is typically comprised of operational results tabulation and reporting, as well as credit, accounts receivable and accounts payable groups. In addition, the accounting group controls the systems the company uses to categorize/allocate money.

It is one thing to follow standards, meet deadlines and accurately complete tasks. Exceptional accountants, however, integrate themselves *and* the business by incorporating workplace communication skills that set new standards. They not only integrate themselves into all areas of the business, they help the business succeed.

Job Expectations & Communication Standards

Understand that you are part of a business team, not just the accounting team.

Too often the accounting group is set apart in their own world whether by self-design or management-design. This should not be the case. Your reporting and analysis is vital to the company's infrastructure, and you should take every opportunity to incorporate your activity into the rest of the organization. The first step is embracing this philosophy for yourself, the next is incorporating it into every interaction you have with other departments in the company.

Know that the system can & should be modified to meet the business's needs.

There are reporting standards that must be met, but in addition to that, know that rigid structures can and should accommodate the needs of each department so that the data is understandable and useable for the organization. The more capable you are at making accommodations for coding and system reports, the more valuable you will become to the company. Do this in collaboration with department heads throughout the business. Tweaking things here and there is not the answer; instead, work together to agree to a set of changes that are understood and useful to all parties. Plan the changes, launch them and ensure they are adding value.

Ensure AP/AR employees act for the benefit of the company.

Customers are not owned by sales, they are owned by every individual including accounts payable, receivable and the credit department. That means that customer service needs to be aligned in all areas of the business. Hand-offs to other departments to settle issues is not the answer, collaboration is. Make sure there is positive communication between departments and that the customer is always front and center.

Align yourself with management at all levels.

Set up meetings with both senior and middle managers in the organization. Present your current reporting tools to them in very simplistic terms. Make cheat sheets for them so that they understand the reports that are being presented in a way that non-accountants can understand the meaning behind the numbers. This may even mean changing acronyms to real descriptions so they can understand. By establishing a good relationship with individuals throughout the organization, you will not only be more appreciated, you will have a better appreciation for the value you are bringing to the team.

Understand the data you are reporting.

Too often checks and balances are just that, numbers in the system. If you don't understand the meaning behind the numbers, how can you present the data and help the organization understand them too? You will benefit by asking questions while helping others to understand.

Create useful reporting tools linked to the business strategy.

Have you thought about creating reports that compare how departments are spending money, or reports that are linked to cost cutting measures with goals vs. actual results each month? What about providing overtime-spending reports by department, or sales expenses for each sales region? Raw material purchase price comparisons month over month, or how about operating costs per product line? These reports can come from the accounting group instead of each area of business trying to run their own reports that are never linked to actual company results. Avoid month end comparison arguments, and start working as a team.

CUSTOMER SERVICE

Shared Mindset

Customer Service is the attitude, responsiveness & resource an organization provides to its customer throughout the buying cycle. Customer service is the front line interface between the company and the customer, providing an advocate for the customer while maintaining company policy and strategic focus. Communication is typically directed via a call center, store location or online. Customer service issues include order entry, quality complaints, and questions pertaining to an existing order, product recommendations, returns and other miscellaneous concerns. Although most companies rely on a specific department to define customer service, it should be a part of everyone's role in the organization to support the attitude projected to increase a customer's satisfaction level.

No matter what position you hold in the organization, customer service should be part of your job.

Job Expectations & Communication Standards

Understand your products.

If you are in Customer Service, you are first person a customer talks to, so you need to be able to answer the majority of their questions, not just pass the question on to someone else in the company. Ask for product training. If there is no formal or extensive training program, align yourself with a sales person to get a more in depth knowledge of the company's products. It will make your customers happy and you will have more confidence in your job. Take the time to create your own product-training manual, have others look at it and add/make modifications.

Remain customer focused.

Have you ever experienced a customer service person that seems annoyed that you are asking them a question? This is not customer focused! Imagine yourself as the customer, how would you want to be treated? Listen to them, keep a smile on your face and project your interest in helping them find solutions. Try putting a mirror on your desk and check out the expression you are giving to your customer.

Proactively manage personalities.

Learning to manage different personalities both internally and externally can be difficult. One way is to take a deep breath and an open mind into every dialog you have. Another is to proactively train yourself on different personality types. Document the interactions you have with difficult people and define how you could have handled yourself better. What would you do the next time you encounter someone like that? If you study personality types and your responses to them, you will be able to proactively manage the situation better and provide better service the next time you encounter a similar situation. Remember to keep ego out of it. Being humble and resourceful is a better approach.

Maintain quality control and attention to detail.

Mistakes happen, but it is your job to minimize the potential for those mistakes by providing and receiving ongoing training on the systems and processes used in your job. You should consider implementing a documented quality control system such as an ISO system that accounts for standardized practices for customer service, as well as how to handle quality complaints and customer disputes. By putting a system like this in place you are not only self-auditing and training to make improvements, but you are standardizing the service level to ensure the entire team is held to the same standards and practices. This attention to detail will raise the overall reputation of service in your organization.

Know the strengths and weaknesses of your team.

Nobody is great at everything, but some of us are definitely better than others at some things. If you are managing a customer service group, it is important to know what each person is great at doing. Don't be afraid to rearrange workload to take advantage of these strengths, pay premiums for them and use them as a model to train others. Some examples are expediting, international customers, returns, quality concerns, and key accounts. In some cases you can funnel these items through key people, in others, you can have them oversee the group activity and focus on universal improvements; stepping in to assist when necessary.

Track your results.

Often the customer service group is taken for granted by other areas of the organization. As a result the responsiveness of the organization to customer service/customer issues is not as timely as required. By tracking your results and establishing a group of result metrics, you have an opportunity to target problem areas, amplify the customer's needs and engage your entire organization in service level accountability.

Some examples of metrics include:

- Number of orders vs. number of returns

- Dollar value of returns vs. sales dollars by month

- Response time from operations on quality complaints

- Reason for complaint broken out by category such as late delivery, quality problem, wrong product shipped, out of stock product, data entry error

First track results, next share them, and finally, facilitate improvement plans.

FINANCE

Shared Mindset

Finance is a service organization. The service it provides is the gathering, reporting & interpretation of data: financials, budgets, investments and expenditures, as well as economic projections. It is finance's role to create and provide financial models to ensure a consistency for decision-making in the organization. In addition to financial modeling, it is finance's responsibility to structure financial resources to meet business demands for investment in projects or support negotiations where investment is required.

Finance is an incredibly important aspect of any business. So important that many companies make the mistake of shielding it from daily operations & functional managers. This leads to ignorance, animosity, wasted time and resources as managers make investment requests that get denied. By proactively teaching and integrating financial decision processes throughout the organization, Finance Professionals can redefine their role as gatekeeper, building a more efficient organization where more timely decisions are made with a higher likelihood of approval.

Job Expectations & Communication Standards

Understand the needs of your organization, not just your boss.

Every area of the company spends money; decisions are being made every day. Just because money is budgeted does not mean it is a good investment. You can help everyday decision makers ensure their thought process is in line with the company's benefit in mind. Learn the different areas of your organization, talk with people and explain to them what you look at verses what they look at. Establish if there is something you can do to help them justify their spending, or pricing in the case of sales negotiations.

Create useful tools and ensure those who use them understand them.

Whether it is a capital equipment purchase, a contract price negotiation, an equity investment in a joint venture or preparing an operational budget, you have the ability to slow down the organization or make it run more efficiently. As long as you create useful tools and properly train people to use them, you will be credited with making things run more efficiently.

Empower people in your company to do an analysis before they bring things to you.

It happens too often that finance professionals are blamed for sitting in their office, looking only at numbers and not understanding the business. The reality is that the people you upset by saying no may not understand the requirements of the business. This is your responsibility to train them in advance. Become a partner to those who seek financial approval. If you proactively work with them, they will be more likely to seek out more justifiable approval, they will know what the company is requiring and will be more likely to ask for your support to help them structure investments. You are a gatekeeper, not a roadblock and it is your responsibility to provide this support to the organization.

Align yourself with Executive Leadership.

Understand the strategic plans of your executive team, and ensure that your services and messages to the workforce are aligned.

Proactively conduct external and internal research.

Know what is happening in your industry, how deals are being structured. Do an analysis of pricing and costing structures and help determine how competitive your organization is in comparison. Research and report economic trends. Share your results throughout your organization and you will become a greater resource to the company.

Track your results.

How many capital expenditure requests were submitted vs. approved? What are the statistics for all other aspects of your approvals? This analysis will help guide you to the areas where you need to focus on training and providing better tools.

HUMAN RESOURCES

Shared Mindset

Human Resources is a service organization. The service it provides is the company's stability system. It is HR's responsibility to ensure compatible talent enters the organization in a motivating and supportive environment, and that incompatible talent leaves the organization in a timely and fair/lawful manner. Ensuring success requires an oversight of all people and processes to enable a balance of progressive growth for individual employees, the overall workforce and the management team.

Human Resources is a tough job, and often underappreciated. Employees complain that HR does not do enough to help their job growth. Managers complain that they have to do everything themselves. Human Resource professionals complain that they get pulled into everything too late to have any impact. The communication flow in and out of Human Resources, as described below, is crucial in overcoming these complaints.

Job Expectations & Communication Standards

Know the people who work in your company and have them know you.

Too often Human Resource personnel know employees on paper, but not in person. One way to achieve a productive and mutual relationship is to ensure employees know you as well. This interaction will create a confidence and trust which is essential for developing a culture of accountability. You can do this by designating one hour a day to conduct meetings for employees that set up appointments with you, and one hour for you to conduct appointments you establish with random employees. The constant flow of talent will encourage positive dialog and diffuse any fear of being called into the HR office! If you set the ground rules for these discussions, they will not be sessions to complain, but sessions to be constructive about professional growth. Limit discussions to 10-15 minutes to ensure positive dialog, and document interactions so you can follow up.

Know the supervisors and managers in your company.

These are the people that are entrusted with the livelihood of the company. Many times they have not had formal training or they just need support and don't want to ask for it. If you make it a point to meet with them one on one a few times a year to help them be better at professional development, you will both benefit from the experience. Remember to keep a consistent message. Your goal is to have a consistency in the experience employees have with their supervisors; this will build a more fulfilling and productive company culture. It will also help you when bringing in new talent.

Know what your company does.

You must have a good understanding of your company's products or services, as well as how the products or services are produced and managed. Without this knowledge you cannot properly acquire compatible talent. It is not enough to leave it to the hiring manager, take the time to learn so that you can properly vet candidates.

Align yourself with Executive Leadership.

Understand the strategic plans of the executive team, and ensure that your services and messages to the workforce are aligned. Unfortunately many times HR is brought in too late; it is your responsibility to ensure this is not the case. The more tapped into the company you are on an ongoing basis, the more likely executive leadership will rely on you in the beginning. This same principle applies to your relationships with functional managers as well.

Proactively conduct external and internal research.

Know the hiring practices and pay policies in the industry and in the local community, compare them to your own. Participate in local organizations that will enable you to share data. Create a network of headhunters, lawyers, union negotiators (if you are unionized), benefit providers, as well as HR professionals in the area, so that you have support and resources to pull from when you need it. Also know the training programs that are available. If you get management buy-in in advance for "approved" programs, you will be able to have a qualified list of training that will be easier to implement on a more proactive basis.

Track your results.

You are spending money on training, payroll, consultants, lawyers, benefits etc. You should be able to tie this spending to the success of the company. Share these results with Executive Leadership and you will most likely get more support for your actions. You should also share your results with managers who can cheerlead for your cause. When they see the value of your efforts, they will push to fund your projects because of the impact it has on their own team.

There are countless things Human Resource professionals do in their day-to-day, however lack of communication with employees and other department managers is often the cause of misunderstanding and frustration. By using these six communication tactics, HR professionals can proactively improve their alignment with others in the organization. It is also useful for professionals outside of HR to understand these skills and initiate dialog to improve their own relationship with the HR team.

INFORMATION TECHNOLOGY

Shared Mindset

Information Technology is a service organization. The service it provides is the qualification, installation, customization and support of the company's communications, technology and data infrastructure. It is IT's responsibility to ensure the automation of business processes is functioning and working efficiently. Ensuring success requires a vast knowledge of technology options, how to use and service hardware & software, how to create customized tools, and establish backup systems to provide information security for the overall business.

Let's face it...IT Professionals are not always the most extroverted personalities when it comes to interaction outside of their own department. That can be problematic for them, as well as for the overall success of the company. As a service oriented department, personality and responsiveness are so important, but so is the value their unique and fast paced knowledge can bring. By integrating the Job Expectations and Communication Standards below into their routine, they will be able to integrate their talents into the general population and help lead the organization.

Job Expectations & Communication Standards

Maintain your technology proficiency.

Technology changes every day. Much of your role in IT should be focused on continued training so that you can utilize technology to its fullest capabilities. It is also your role to teach others in the company and support them when they need help. The more trained you are, the more of an asset you will be to the organization. Take advantage of the numerous seminars, training and certification courses available both in classroom settings and online.

Understand industry trends.

Stay educated on industry trends. Find ways to use technology to save the company money, secure data, and improve process efficiencies. What is cool in the IT world does not always transfer into the business wanting to invest. However, if you can prove the value that the technology brings, you will have a better chance of getting your ideas and expenditures approved.

Develop exceptional interpersonal skills.

Each department of the organization has different requirements and your job touches all of them. You will need to learn to communicate at all levels and areas of the organization, with outside contractors and consultants. Too often IT gets a reputation for working in a secluded bubble. If you want to succeed, try to create an environment where you create a reputation of being integrated in each department of the company. Develop good relationships and make an effort to network.

Be patient and become a good listener.

People learn at different speeds, they have different competency levels and different interest levels in technology and programming solutions. Your role is to provide a service, so take the time needed to train people, listen to their concerns and what they want to accomplish. After helping someone, ask if they are satisfied with your work…and listen to their answer.

Understand your company's strategic vision.

Once you understand where the company wants to go, you can better define the tools available to support getting them there. After understanding the overall company strategy, talk to department heads and find out what their needs will be. Work with them in the planning stage for investments in technology. IT is not always part of the planning process, so you need to proactively initiate these discussions and show the value your knowledge of industry trends and internal capabilities brings.

Excel in project management.

Whether you are planning an ERP implementation, migrating to a new operating system, establishing a help desk, upgrading servers, or supporting the launch of an e-commerce system, project management skills are key to your success. Consider taking a class in project management, or getting certified as a PMP (project management professional). It will set you apart as a professional and give you the tools needed to do a better job.

MARKETING & COMMUNICATIONS

Shared Mindset

Marketing is the strategic act of successfully motivating a target market to choose a specific company or product. It is Marketing's responsibility to create an awareness and desire within a group of people that have the means and the need (created or existing) to purchase a product or service. Business Strategy is set here and should flow both externally and internally, meaning it is also Marketing's responsibility to create & communicate the tools and processes for internal use to support the sale of goods.

There is often a stigma around how marketing dollars are spent. Business leaders don't always fully understand marketing programs or how all the elements tie together. Other department heads get frustrated when, in their opinion, investment 'Needs' are turned down, but Marketing still gets funding for 'Wants'. Finally, Marketing Professionals rarely feel they have enough funding for the results everyone expects their programs to achieve. Below are actions the marketing group should be taking to overcome this stigma and achieve desired results.

Job Expectations & Communication Standards

Know your company & have them know you.

Have a deep and documented understanding of the organization, the full breath of products or services, process flows, customer's full cycle buying experience, the product's cost/profit structure and current capabilities. Also have an in-depth understanding of the financials, R&D capabilities &

pipeline. You can't promote something you don't understand, nor can you see practical growth potential without knowing the current reality. Most importantly, share this knowledge throughout all levels of the organization on a continuous basis to ensure they too understand the company's reality.

Why is this important? By doing this your marketing ideas become practical, actionable plans using jargon others, outside of marketing, can understand and support. You will be able to capture low hanging fruit opportunities, and other areas of the company will start to search for those opportunities as well.

Know your current and target customer groups.

Talk to & visit customers, survey customers, understand their buying patterns, both what they buy from the company and what they buy from others *instead* of the company. Know what they like and dislike about the company and its competitors. Understand their full buying *experience* and ask them what the company can do better from a service and new product perspective. Find out their future product and service needs. Utilize the sales group when conducting ongoing studies, work with them and have them help you. Document & analyze your results, then share your analysis throughout the organization.

Why is this important? Talking directly with current and potential customers is eye opening, especially when you are *not* trying to sell them anything. Customers tend to open up and share valuable information during this dialog because, in the end, they may gain something from it. Marketing professionals that collect this data, compile it and share results, trends, and opportunities with sales and the rest of the organization, can build internal support for their programs.

Know your competitors.

Research & document competitor products and services, understand why customers buy from them and why they don't buy from them. Try to determine the company's prices compared to theirs. Understand their target markets, their strengths and weaknesses. Document their process flows & customer experience (you can do this by buying from them, or talking with their customers). Your sales team can and should help you with this. Put your objectives together and establish a tactical plan together with sales.

Why is this important? There is no need to recreate the wheel. If a competitor is doing something well, you should learn from them. If they are doing something poorly, you can learn what not to do. Also, it gives you an opportunity to direct the organization into a strategic sweet spot. The more you understand the competitor's capabilities vs. the company's, you can adapt your message, development efforts and marketing dollars toward an area of opportunity where the organization can be unique.

Know & plan your marketing tools.

Whether it be PR, advertising, websites, presentations, literature, DVD's, direct marketing, trade shows, sales tools, packaging, product launches, social media, etc...you don't have to do them all. Your importance is not based on your marketing budget, it is based on the growth you bring to the company by *effectively* spending as little as possible to achieve business & strategic goals.

Why is this important? If you take this philosophical approach to planning and spending, others will be able to understand the value of your programs as you explain your methodology. Ambiguous fund allocation such as brand building is often difficult to sell internally. However, if you couple the long-term/ambiguous budget requests with short and medium term effective spending strategies, you will increase your chances of getting budget support.

Proactively lead your internal and external strategy.

By doing market and internal research, and by understanding the company's internal organization, you can create a comprehensive strategy and implementation plan that the *entire* company can embrace. Analyze data points, find strengths and weakness, opportunities and threats, define where the company is today in the competitive mix and where it can move to in the marketplace. Define internally changes and with products and services that need to be made in order to reach strategic opportunities. Most importantly, get buy-in from all levels and areas of the organization. Your information, analysis and proposal are paramount for executive leadership to set the course and fund the execution. The integration and collaboration of all business functions will ensure sustainable success. Be proactive.

Why is this important? Integrated marketing approaches are successful marketing approaches. They provide the opportunity to lead the organization, align investment dollars, as well as functional activities to achieve goals. Waiting for budget time to present a plan is a setup for failure, especially in this economic time when percentage of revenue budget allocations are not always feasible. A proactive approach to marketing strategy is something everyone can buy into because you work hard to ensure all aspects are understood and make sense for the business.

Track your results.

You are spending a lot of money, document where it goes, how much is spent, the objective you are trying to achieve and the sales result. Results should be tracked monthly, quarterly and annually. If your actions are not showing the result you need, change them....you have a lot of tools to pick from. Link your spending to your strategy and this will lead to success.

Why is this important? Too often marketing takes all the credit for growth; this leads to animosity in the organization. By sharing the work, the knowledge, the results and the credit, you will be able to drive the organization and funding for future marketing efforts.

Don't forget to share your results. The result belongs to everyone.

OPERATIONS

Shared Mindset

Operations, Logistics & Engineering are three key areas of the business model that function to get the company's products developed, produced and distributed. Often relying solely on the input of other business areas for product requirements, volumes & pricing, the Operations, Logistics & Engineering (OL&E) group must focus on meeting demand while continuously improving processes, quality, costs and timing. Whether it is a manufacturing company, service provider or retail environment, the OL&E group is vital to the company's short and long-term success, requires significant capital investment and manages the majority of company personnel.

As market dynamics change, so should your operations group. Make sure you are proactive, able to adapt, and stay competitive. Here are six success tips all operations professionals should incorporate into their routine.

Job Expectations & Communication Standards

Focus on Communication input and output.

Often times operations becomes a microcosm of its own and loses touch unintentionally, sometimes deliberately, with the rest of the organization. Don't let this happen. Be open to market demands and listen to the customer both internally and externally. Understand the company's overall strategy and incorporate it into the operations world. Spread the message and allow your employees to understand how their job is part of the big picture; quality will improve, morale will improve. The better a communicator you are, the more likely you will get capital approvals as well.

Engage with your employees.

Great people skills will provide an advantage when the operation needs to be flexible. Listen to your employees; provide ongoing training and consistent feedback. Address performance concerns quickly and resolve disputes by focusing on what is right, not who is right.

Maintain useful metrics and an analytical mindset.

There are two types of metrics to track: The first group of metrics is used to manage the operation including production quantity, scrap levels, product costs, raw materials, lead-times, safety reports, quality claims/complaints, shipping performance, machine speeds, etc...This is a very large group of metrics and must be reviewed on a consistent basis in order to micromanage each area and ensure the performance of the operation. However, there is a second group of metrics. This group consists of metrics linked to the overall business strategy: where you are today and what you need to achieve to be successful. This group probably has some elements that you are already tracking in the first group of metrics, but it has others as well. For example: Key customer lead-time reductions, inventory turns on new product lines, cost savings/earned profit from reduction of product returns. Share your metrics throughout the organization, make them proactive and create an analytical mindset in everything you do.

Stay on top of trends in equipment and engineering.

You and your team should be aware of new technologies, as well as have the ability to improve on the existing technology you are utilizing. Technology dictates speed, quality, innovation and in many cases, service levels. Many companies fail because they don't adapt to changing market trends. Go to trade shows, read technical papers, and participate in professional and industry specific associations. If you manage technology and improve your technical knowledge, you will have an edge over the competition.

Be Flexible.

Creating a balance between controlling the process and being flexible is always a difficult concept, especially if you are tracking your metrics, or tied to an automated process. However, business is competitive and you need to ensure that Operations, Logistics and Engineering can adapt to changing market conditions. One approach is to create a subset environment for flexibility - "loophole management" if you will. If you track this activity you may find that market demands are growing for these changes and you may need to re-engineer your process to make a new common practice. By creating this subset environment, the day-to-day will not be disrupted by change; instead you will manage it and be proactive about it.

Implement a continuous improvement philosophy in everything you do.

There are so many techniques for continuous improvement these days, whether you bring in consultants, you or your employees become certified, read books or utilize various "Lean" and "Six Sigma" tools, whatever you do, make sure that the philosophy to improve is in everything you do.

Conduct best practice reviews and get feedback from the organization on new ways/areas to implement these concepts; reward improvements by posting successes and communicating results.

PROJECT MANAGEMENT

Shared Mindset

Project Management is the act of leading a company initiative that typically has a start date, end date, specific funding constraints and deliverables. The Project Manager is essentially the General Manager of the company initiative, responsible for planning the full cycle of the project, defining and achieving milestones, managing the budget, securing funding, defining the scope, negotiating, securing and organizing internal and external resources, as well as problem solving. Project Managers must be very organized and systematic, they need to lead and manage various groups of resources that are strained by competing deliverables. In addition, they are responsible for profit and loss for the project. Some examples of projects include setting up a new retail store location, building a new factory or new house construction, defining & commissioning new manufacturing equipment, or choosing and implementing new ERP or CRM systems.

Job Expectations & Communication Standards

Manage your risks in advance.

As Project Manager you will be responsible for securing resources, which means negotiating contracts with many external and internal groups. Make sure you take the time to write the scope of work for each contractor with the amount of detail necessary to ensure the work gets done according to your schedule and criteria. Include exit clauses and penalties if the scope is not met to your satisfaction.

Communicate early and often.

Typically there are several stakeholders in a project including those you report to and those reporting to you. Communicate your plan from the beginning of the project. Set expectations and keep everyone informed as to the milestones, status, lessons learned, and budget to actual. It is your job to ensure everyone's interests are aligned at all times.

Utilize the PMP skill set.

If you have not already received your Project Management Professional Certification, put your plan in place to understand the principles, using them in your everyday transactions and working toward certification. It is not only a self-improvement activity, but fundamental real-world tools to help you become better at your job including time management, project charting, organizational and communication tools, etc....

Identify what is important to achieving success.

Take the time to identify and agree to the scope of the project with all stakeholders prior to defining your resources, timeline or budget. Ensure that objectives are clear and attainable and everyone shares the definition of what is important. By doing this you will be better able to adapt when needed throughout the project timeline while maintaining the integrity of the project.

Understand financing and budgeting.

You are not only responsible for managing the project budget, but most likely you are responsible for planning it, funding it, tracking it and reporting on costs and profitability. If you do not have a background in accounting or finance, you should take the time to understand these processes as they pertain to your project and the company you are working for. You can do this by taking courses in project finance, accounting & project management, investigating project management software, and reading books on the subject. You can also sit down with the accounting or finance departments and have them guide you through the process that they would like to see. A hybrid approach to learning will ensure you provide what is needed for others along with the tools you need to manage the project most effectively.

Own the schedule.

It is your responsibility to create and manage the schedule. With so many elements to consider, flexibility and schedule optimization are imperative to your success of ultimately meeting the deadline for the project. Be prepared and stay on top of each and every element of the project. By doing this you can make changes, and shift timelines within your master plan. Utilize project management software, making your schedule visual; this will help you to communicate and track activities with your project team. Always track the actual dates compared to your initial plan for the project. Keep track of milestones throughout the project. This will give you a chance to modify dates to accomplish intermediate deadlines, rather than shifting the end deadline for the project. If something did not happen as planned, conduct a "lessons learned" review with your team. Understand what went wrong, and how to avoid it happening at any other stage of the project. Always keep your visual project timeline updated and review it often with your team. Establishing a regular review such as once a week is a good way to keep up momentum for your project.

PURCHASING & SUPPLY CHAIN

Shared Mindset

Purchasing/Procurement & Supply Chain Management is an activity integral to the competitiveness of an organization. In order to be cost effective, the operations team requires materials to arrive just-in-time to avoid spending money too long before the product can be sold, it also requires competitive pricing on all consumables meeting specific quality standards in order to produce products that can be sold at a specific profit level. In addition to managing procurement of items to meet those requirements, typical job activities include establishing & qualifying multiple sources for procurement, managing relationships and researching competitive pricing, coordinating outbound transportation services and proactively negotiating to improve efficiencies and services to ensure a better cost position for the company.

Job Expectations & Communication Standards

Never discount the importance of relationships.

Building great relationships, both internal and external, will help you facilitate successful negotiations. Take the time to understand the needs of the company, whether it is those of your operations group, new product development team, accounting team, or logistics organization. All have different needs that you will have to consider when evaluating suppliers. Don't wait until problems occur, have an ongoing dialog with all internal groups so that you are providing the best products and services to them. These internal relationships will give you more leverage as you build your external supplier relationships. You will be viewed as a more credible and creative negotiator.

Saving money should not always be the top priority.

Pricing, quality requirements, delivery requirements, backup planning, volume management, packaging, financial stability and R&D capabilities are among the many aspects that make a viable supplier. If your focus is only on saving money, you may be missing out on making your company more profitable. Understand how each product is used and where costs and profits lie within the operational chain of the organization. You may find that paying a higher purchase price for an item that is customized to meet the needs of the operational chain can generate a lower cost product and higher profits for the company.

Understand current product and service rates.

Having the ability to go to a supplier and say "this is what we need and what we will pay for it" will give you an advantage only if you have a good understanding of the competitive rates in the market. You should understand regional and industry wide rates for all aspects of the company's procurement needs.

Know your suppliers, not just their sales agents.

Make it a point to have regular visits with suppliers at their facilities, understand their capabilities, and know the people within their organization that can make decisions. It is also a good idea to bring your quality personnel with you to conduct regular audits of their operation. The more integrated you become with suppliers, the more demanding you can be with them.

Building consensus can be challenging but rewarding.

Many times members within the organization may be committed to using a supplier for the wrong reasons, often due to a long prior relationship. Just because they are content, does not mean it is in the best interest of the company to stay with them. Changing suppliers is difficult, but if you approach it by consensus building you will find that change is not only obtainable, but also welcomed. Work as a team internally to itemize services required, at the same time bring to the table services that are offered in the industry. Put a dream list together at a target price point and let suppliers come in to pitch their offers to the team. By including everyone in the process you will not only get internal buy-in, but you will get suppliers to put more into their offers knowing that the decision is collaborative.

Understand contract design standards within your industry.

Although creativity within your own contracts can bring you a competitive advantage, you don't want to be the only customer scrambling for product when a shortage occurs because your competitors have contracted aspects of supply agreements that yours does not have. Talk with various suppliers in the industry and find out what the norms are for contract design. Make sure your creativity in negotiating is above and beyond these standards.

QUALITY & SAFETY

Shared Mindset

The Quality and Safety department's primary focus is to ensure products and services meet customer expectations, while the processes used to create them are safe for all employees. In many companies, these departments are combined -- since the tools used by its professionals require expertise in root cause analysis and corrective action. A well-managed Quality and Safety department creates value in an organization by eliminating waste and errors, reducing workplace accidents and ultimately improving productivity. Positions within these departments typically report through operations directors. Increasingly, however, more-progressive companies are creating straight-line reporting structures to general management and executive-level decision-makers. These new organizational structures foster better accountability and remove any conflict of interest for front-line managers.

There are two common organizational flaws in quality and safety *programs*. The first is the company that goes out of its way to preach the importance of quality and safety, but does not back it up with an infrastructure that establishes metrics and systems to continuously improve. Second is the company that has an internal group of individuals trying to make a difference, but does not have the management commitment to measure qualified metrics as a means of judging success. Below are some actions you can take to ensure quality and safety *programs* are living and breathing *cross-functional continuous improvement initiatives* that determine your company's success.

Job Expectations & Communication Standards

Have documented procedures and "Standard Work" for all processes.

Good quality processes start with documented procedures and standardized work instructions. If done well, they are brief, easy to read and taught to multiple employees. Good "Standard Work" is often pictorial in nature and can be summarized in single page printouts. The same applies to all safety procedures. Employees need to be able to refer to these documents at their point of work whether in the office, on the shop floor, or in the field.

Consider hiring skilled professionals with backgrounds in Lean, Six Sigma and Quality Management.

Most organizations understand when they have poor quality, and they certainly know when there is a safety problem. But few understand the scientific tools used to correct and improve performance in both. The "science" of quality and safety has been developed for decades by professionals from some of the best companies in the world. An entire industry of quality experts commonly use tools such as Six Sigma to control their processes, or "Lean" – to reduce waste and non value-added steps in their daily work. Choosing the right tool depends on the type of problem an organization is having. A good Quality Manager is well schooled in several of these paradigms and chooses the right tool for the job – without over-applying any specific discipline.

Have key decision-makers develop a series of top-line metrics for measurement.

It is often said, "you can't manage what you can't measure." All quality and safety processes require good metrics to baseline current performance, set targets for future improvement, and understand when things have changed. All metrics start with a good value statement – "What is the customer (both internal or external) willing to pay or give for the output of the process being affected?" Metrics – or measurements – allow the owners of processes to fully understand if they are delivering the value expected by the customer. All levels of an organization need at least 3-5 key metrics to monitor performance.

Develop a safety and quality mission statement and culture.

Every organization – large or small – needs to have a vision and mission if they want the organization to perform and succeed. In larger organizations, a formal, written statement of these values is often required to ensure that all employees are reached with the message. But writing a mission statement and *posting* it on a conference room wall is not enough to build a great organizational culture – especially in Quality and Safety. All great companies must have its leadership "walk the talk" of quality and safety at all levels. Metrics, tools and accountability help build that culture, but good people make it come to life.

Recruit champions in each area of your business.

Promote your cause throughout the organization by training someone in each department to implement and influence continuous improvement activities in their area. These individuals will champion and lead by example as your message gets spread. Make sure that all members of the senior management team back this project and support their employee's participation.

Share your results.

Create a monthly newsletter or email that reiterates your objectives for the company, as well as gives accolades to those people and departments that are implementing continuous improvement actions. Use it as a vehicle to share ideas and results in layman's terms while raising the profile of your cause throughout the company.

You don't have to work in any particular department to measure quality or safety. You can and should be proactive about measuring your own results and the results of your team.

SALES

Shared Mindset

Sales is the act of convincing someone to choose you. That could be choosing you over someone else, it could be choosing you because you planted a new idea in someone's head and they chose to follow you, or it could be that you have something that meets a specific need and they sought you out. No matter what the catalyst, sales is the result, the act, the decision, the final choice...being you.

Typically there are personality traits used to describe a good sales person: outgoing, thoughtful, positive, responsive, knowledgeable, etc.... Although personality traits are very important, there are some other traits to look for, develop and focus on to succeed in sales. These traits are listed below.

Job Expectations & Communication Standards

Take it personally.

When you take things personally, you hold yourself accountable. By holding yourself accountable you:

- Become the go-to person.

- Become the expert.

- Become more passionate about what you are selling.

When you take it personally, people will trust you and believe in you.

Be resourceful.

No buyer wants to think that his or her dollar stops with you. You need to represent the product, the company, and actually have all areas of the company backing you. Too many sales people *act* as if this is the case, make promises to customers, then go on to complain when promises can't be upheld. That can't be you. If you are going to succeed, you need to buck up, and make connections throughout all levels and silos of the organization, develop them as resources for your customer, and be able to follow through. Hint...humility goes a long way.

Become a teacher.

If you are to succeed, you need to teach. The more you know about your product or service, the better you can represent it to your prospective customers and to your prospective internal resources. The more you know and share, the more people will follow you and support you. Find creative ways to do this. Ask to hold a meeting with different departments or individuals in the company, share what you know, ask for input on how you can collectively improve. You will be surprised how little people know about the products they make and how little you know about what it really takes to support you. This learning experience will educate all of you, and as a team, you will sell more.

Analyze your failures.

When you take things personally, it's difficult not to get upset when you don't get the sale. Don't get upset, do the analysis, share it with your internal resources and move forward together. No matter how good you think you are, you can always improve; this is one way of doing it. Your ability to move forward and become better is all part of holding yourself accountable.

Create growth.

Managing an account base is not enough, nor is prospecting for new customers. The two must go hand in hand or growth will not happen. True success of a sales person is to increase the number of customers and the total dollars earned from all customers current and new. Know your product, your customers, your internal resources, your competitors, your target growth areas and your results.

Track your results.

So many sales people track their success based upon their actions, not their results...Companies fail because of this and sales people lose their jobs without knowing what hit them. Become results oriented, share your results internally and give credit to the entire team.

V
THE CROSS FUNCTIONAL BUSINESS SURVEY

How Cross Functional is Your Business?

From your perspective…how well does each functional business area work?

ACCOUNTING

1. We have a Shared Mindset of Accounting across the *entire* business.

Do Well _____   Needs Improvement _____

Why this does not apply _____

The Accounting Group...

2. Understands that Accounting is part of a business team, not just the accounting team.

Do Well _____   Needs Improvement _____

Why this does not apply _____

3. Knows that the system can and should be modified to meet the business's needs.

Do Well _____   Needs Improvement _____

Why this does not apply _____

4. Ensures AP/AR employees act for the benefit of the company.

Do Well _____   Needs Improvement _____

Why this does not apply _____

5. Aligns itself with management of all levels.

Do Well _____   Needs Improvement _____

Why this does not apply _____

6. Understands the data being reported.

Do Well _____   Needs Improvement _____

Why this does not apply _____

7. Creates useful reporting tools linked to the business strategy.

Do Well _____   Needs Improvement _____

Why this does not apply _____

CUSTOMER SERVICE

1. We have a Shared Mindset of Customer Service across the *entire* business.

Do Well _____   Needs Improvement _____

Why this does not apply _____

The Customer Service Group...

2. Understands all products.

Do Well _____   Needs Improvement _____

Why this does not apply _____

3. Remains customer focused.

Do Well _____   Needs Improvement _____

Why this does not apply _____

4. Proactively manages personalities.

Do Well _____   Needs Improvement _____

Why this does not apply _____

5. Maintains quality control and attention to detail.

Do Well _____   Needs Improvement _____

Why this does not apply _____

6. Knows the strengths & weaknesses of the team.

Do Well _____   Needs Improvement _____   Why this does not apply

_____

7. Tracks results, shares them and facilitates improvement plans.

Do Well _____   Needs Improvement _____   Why this does not apply

_____

FINANCE

1. We have a Shared Mindset of Finance across the *entire* business.

Do Well _____   Needs Improvement _____

Why this does not apply _____

The Finance Group...

2. Understands the needs of the organization, not just their boss.

Do Well _____   Needs Improvement _____

Why this does not apply _____

3. Creates useful tools to ensure those who use them understand them.

Do Well _____   Needs Improvement _____

Why this does not apply _____

4. Empowers people in the company to do an analysis before bringing requests to Finance.

Do Well _____   Needs Improvement _____

Why this does not apply _____

5. Aligns itself with Executive Leadership.

Do Well _____   Needs Improvement _____

Why this does not apply _____

6. Understands the data being reported.

Do Well _____   Needs Improvement _____

Why this does not apply _____

7. Proactively conducts external and internal research.

Do Well _____   Needs Improvement _____

Why this does not apply _____

8. Tracks results to determine where to focus training and provide better tools.

Do Well _____   Needs Improvement _____

Why this does not apply _____

HUMAN RESOURCES

1. We have a Shared Mindset of Human Resources across the *entire* business.

Do Well _____   Needs Improvement _____

Why this does not apply _____

The Human Resources Group...

2. Knows all company employees and makes an effort to be known by them.

Do Well _____   Needs Improvement _____

Why this does not apply _____

3. Knows the supervisors and managers throughout the company.

Do Well _____   Needs Improvement _____

Why this does not apply _____

4. Knows what the company does.

Do Well _____   Needs Improvement _____

Why this does not apply _____

5. Aligns itself with Executive Leadership.

Do Well _____   Needs Improvement _____

Why this does not apply _____

6. Proactively conducts external and internal research.

Do Well _____   Needs Improvement _____

Why this does not apply _____

7. Tracks & shares results.

Do Well _____   Needs Improvement _____

Why this does not apply _____

INFORMATION TECHNOLOGY

1. We have a Shared Mindset of Information Technology across the *entire* business.

Do Well _____   Needs Improvement _____

Why this does not apply _____

The Information Technology Group…

2. Proactively maintains their technology proficiency.

Do Well _____   Needs Improvement _____

Why this does not apply _____

3. Understands industry trends.

Do Well _____   Needs Improvement _____

Why this does not apply _____

4. Works to develop exceptional interpersonal skills.

Do Well _____   Needs Improvement _____

Why this does not apply _____

5. Exhibits patients and good listening skills.

Do Well _____   Needs Improvement _____

Why this does not apply _____

6. Understands the company's strategic vision.

Do Well _____   Needs Improvement _____

Why this does not apply _____

7. Excels in project management.

Do Well _____   Needs Improvement _____

Why this does not apply _____

MARKETING & COMMUNICATIONS

1. We have a Shared Mindset of Marketing & Communications across the *entire* business.

Do Well _____   Needs Improvement _____

Why this does not apply _____

The Marketing & Communication Group...

2. Knows everyone throughout the company & makes a real effort to be known by everyone.

Do Well _____   Needs Improvement _____

Why this does not apply _____

3. Knows & understands current and target customer groups.

Do Well _____   Needs Improvement _____

Why this does not apply _____

4. Knows and understands competitors.

Do Well _____   Needs Improvement _____

Why this does not apply _____

5. Is aware of and effectively plans the use of marketing tools.

Do Well _____   Needs Improvement _____

Why this does not apply _____

6. Proactively leads the internal and external Marketing & Communications strategy.

Do Well _____   Needs Improvement _____

Why this does not apply _____

7. Tracks results, shares results, gives credit to others and facilitates improvement plans.

Do Well _____   Needs Improvement _____

Why this does not apply _____

OPERATIONS

1. We have a Shared Mindset of Operations across the *entire* business.

Do Well _____   Needs Improvement _____

Why this does not apply _____

The Operations Group...

2. Exhibits a real focus on communication input and output.

Do Well _____   Needs Improvement _____

Why this does not apply _____

3. Management is engaged with all employees.

Do Well _____   Needs Improvement _____

Why this does not apply _____

4. Maintains useful metrics and an analytical mindset.

Do Well _____   Needs Improvement _____

Why this does not apply _____

5. Stays on top of trends in equipment and engineering.

Do Well _____   Needs Improvement _____

Why this does not apply _____

6. Is flexible when needed.

Do Well _____   Needs Improvement _____

Why this does not apply _____

7. Implements a continuous improvement philosophy in everything they do.

Do Well _____   Needs Improvement _____

Why this does not apply _____

PROJECT MANAGEMENT

1. We have a Shared Mindset of Project Management across the *entire* business.

Do Well _____   Needs Improvement _____

Why this does not apply _____

The Project Management Group...

2. Manages risks in advance.

Do Well _____   Needs Improvement _____

Why this does not apply _____

3. Communicates early and often.

Do Well _____   Needs Improvement _____

Why this does not apply _____

4. Utilizes the PMP skill set.

Do Well _____   Needs Improvement _____

Why this does not apply _____

5. Identifies what is important to achieving success.

Do Well _____   Needs Improvement _____

Why this does not apply _____

6. Understands financing and budgeting.

Do Well _____   Needs Improvement _____

Why this does not apply _____

7. Owns the schedule.

Do Well _____   Needs Improvement _____

Why this does not apply _____

PURCHASING & SUPPLY CHAIN

1. We have a Shared Mindset of Purchasing & Supply Chain across the *entire* business.

Do Well _____   Needs Improvement _____

Why this does not apply _____

The Purchasing & Supply Chain Group...

2. Never discounts the importance of relationships.

Do Well _____   Needs Improvement _____

Why this does not apply _____

3. Understands that saving money is not always the top priority.

Do Well _____   Needs Improvement _____

Why this does not apply _____

4. Understands current industry product and service rates.

Do Well _____   Needs Improvement _____

Why this does not apply _____

5. Thoroughly knows suppliers, not just their sales agents.

Do Well _____   Needs Improvement _____

Why this does not apply _____

6. Builds consensus on decisions.

Do Well _____   Needs Improvement _____

Why this does not apply _____

7. Understands contract design standards within the industry.

Do Well _____   Needs Improvement _____

Why this does not apply _____

QUALITY & SAFETY

1. We have a Shared Mindset of Quality & Safety across the *entire* business.

Do Well _____   Needs Improvement _____

Why this does not apply _____

The Quality & Safety Group...

2. Has documented procedures and "Standard Work" for all processes.

Do Well _____   Needs Improvement _____

Why this does not apply _____

3. Considers hiring skilled professionals with backgrounds in Lean, Six Sigma & Quality Management.

Do Well _____   Needs Improvement _____

Why this does not apply _____

4. Has key decision-makers develop a series of top-line metrics for measurement.

Do Well _____   Needs Improvement _____

Why this does not apply _____

5. Has developed a safety and quality mission statement and culture.

Do Well _____   Needs Improvement _____

Why this does not apply _____

6. Recruits champions in each area of the business.

Do Well _____   Needs Improvement _____

Why this does not apply _____

7. Shares results.

Do Well _____   Needs Improvement _____

Why this does not apply _____

SALES

1. We have a Shared Mindset of Sales across the *entire* business.

Do Well _____   Needs Improvement _____

Why this does not apply _____

The Sales Group...

2. Takes things personally.

Do Well _____   Needs Improvement _____

Why this does not apply _____

3. Is resourceful.

Do Well _____   Needs Improvement _____

Why this does not apply _____

4. Teaches the organization.

Do Well _____   Needs Improvement _____

Why this does not apply _____

5. Analyzes their own failures.

Do Well _____   Needs Improvement _____

Why this does not apply _____

6. Creates overall growth for the business.

Do Well _____   Needs Improvement _____

Why this does not apply _____

7. Tracks & shares meaningful results.

Do Well _____   Needs Improvement _____

Why this does not apply _____

ABOUT THE AUTHOR

 Lisa Woods, President, ManagingAmericans.com & LisaWoodsConsulting.com

Lisa, a thought leader in management and leadership, founded ManagingAmericans.com in 2011 after 20 years successfully leading and driving growth in the corporate world. Her objective is to help mentor and develop professionals to be better leaders, managers, team players and individual contributors in a "do-it-yourself" learning environment using unique & practical tools to support the process. With a B.A. in Corporate Communication and an M.B.A., Lisa's career spans from Global Marketing to General Management and has worked all over the world. Her publications include "4 Essential Skills for Leaders, Managers & High Potentials" © 2013, and "The Cross Functional Business: Beyond Teams" © 2015.

www.ingramcontent.com/pod-product-compliance
Lightning Source LLC
Chambersburg PA
CBHW070843180526
45168CB00002B/941